DOT COMPLIANCE ESSENTIALS

Be Audit Ready

Dobbs Media

Table of Contents

1. Driver Qualification Files (DQFs)

Ensure all drivers have valid Commercial Driver's Licenses (CDLs):

Importance: CDLs are essential for commercial drivers, as they certify that the driver has the necessary skills and knowledge to operate commercial motor vehicles (CMVs) safely.

Procedure: Regularly check and verify that all drivers in your fleet possess a valid CDL. This involves reviewing the CDL's expiration date and class, ensuring it covers the types of vehicles they operate, and checking for any endorsements required for specific cargo or vehicle types.

Verify that drivers meet DOT medical requirements and maintain up-to-date medical certificates:

Importance: DOT medical requirements are in place to ensure that drivers are physically and mentally fit for the demands of commercial driving, promoting safety on the road.

Procedure: Each driver should undergo a DOT-compliant medical examination conducted by a certified medical examiner. Ensure that the medical examiner issues a valid Medical Examiner's Certificate (commonly known as a "DOT medical card"). Keep copies of these certificates and regularly check their expiration dates to ensure drivers remain compliant.

Confirm that all drivers have completed a driver's application and been properly screened for qualifications:

Importance: The driver's application is a critical document that provides essential information about a driver's qualifications and work history, helping employers make informed hiring decisions.

Procedure: Create a standardized driver application form that collects comprehensive information, including employment history, driving history, accidents, traffic violations, and previous employer references. Ensure that all new hires complete this application. Additionally, conduct background checks, including driving records and criminal history checks, as part of your screening process.

Maintain records of driver histories, including employment verifications, drug and alcohol testing, and previous employer checks:

Importance: Keeping thorough records of driver histories helps ensure that you have qualified and safe drivers on your team while demonstrating compliance with DOT regulations.

Procedure:

- Employment Verifications: Document past employment history for each driver, including contact information for previous employers, dates of employment, and job responsibilities.
- Drug and Alcohol Testing: Maintain records of pre-employment, random, post-accident, and reasonable suspicion drug and alcohol tests. This includes documenting test results, the testing facility, and dates.
- Previous Employer Checks: Reach out to previous employers for reference checks, especially for the last three years of employment. Verify the driver's safety

performance, accidents, and drug and alcohol violations, if any.

General Tips:

- Create a dedicated file or digital database for each driver to organize and store these records securely.
- Keep all records in compliance with DOT regulations, including record retention periods.
- Regularly review and update DQFs to ensure all information is current and accurate.
- Be prepared to provide these records during a DOT audit or upon request by authorities.
- Consider implementing a driver management software system to help streamline record-keeping and compliance tracking.

By diligently following these procedures and maintaining comprehensive DQFs, your organization can demonstrate compliance with DOT regulations and ensure that your drivers are qualified and safe for the job.

2. Hours of Service (HOS) Compliance

Ensure all drivers are trained on HOS regulations and maintain accurate logs of their driving hours:

Importance: HOS regulations are designed to prevent driver fatigue and promote road safety by limiting the number of hours a driver can operate a commercial vehicle. Ensuring drivers understand and comply with these rules is crucial.

Procedure:

- Conduct comprehensive HOS training for all drivers during onboarding and periodically thereafter to ensure they understand the rules and can accurately log their hours.

- Emphasize the importance of accurately recording driving, on-duty, and off-duty hours in logbooks or electronic logging devices (ELDs).

- Regularly review and audit driver logs to identify discrepancies, errors, or potential violations.

Review driver logs for violations or inconsistencies:

Importance: Regularly reviewing driver logs helps identify and correct violations before they result in penalties or fines, ensuring compliance and road safety.

Procedure:

- Routinely collect and review driver logs to ensure they accurately reflect hours worked, breaks taken, and rest periods.

- Look for violations such as exceeding daily driving limits, inadequate rest periods, or failing to take required breaks.

- Implement a process for addressing and rectifying any identified violations promptly, including counseling and retraining drivers as necessary.

Verify that drivers have access to required supporting documents (e.g., bills of lading, shipping records) while on the road:

Importance: Drivers must have access to supporting documents that validate their activities and confirm compliance with HOS regulations.

Procedure:

- Ensure that drivers have access to necessary documents such as bills of lading, shipping records, and dispatch instructions.

- Encourage drivers to keep these documents organized and readily accessible to verify their activities during roadside inspections or audits.

Maintain records of exemptions or exceptions to HOS regulations if applicable:

Importance: Some drivers or operations may qualify for exemptions or exceptions to certain HOS regulations. Maintaining records of these exceptions helps demonstrate compliance.

Procedure:

- Identify if any of your drivers or operations qualify for HOS exemptions (e.g., short-haul exemptions, agricultural exemptions).

- Keep records of exemption documentation, such as notifications or waivers, to provide during audits or inspections.

- Ensure that drivers who qualify for exemptions are aware of the specific rules that apply to them and adhere to them accordingly.

General Tips:

- Implement electronic logging devices (ELDs) or electronic logbooks to automate and streamline HOS tracking and compliance.

- Regularly train drivers and staff on any updates or changes to HOS regulations.
- Establish a clear procedure for drivers to report any issues or concerns related to HOS compliance.
- Maintain a record retention system to store HOS-related documents, including driver logs, training records, and exemption documentation.
- Conduct internal audits and mock inspections to proactively identify and correct compliance issues.

By following these procedures and maintaining accurate records, your organization can ensure HOS compliance, reduce the risk of violations, and promote the safety of your drivers and the public on the roads.

3. Vehicle Maintenance and Inspection

Ensure regular vehicle maintenance and inspections are performed as per DOT regulations:

Importance: Regular maintenance and inspections are critical for ensuring the safe operation of commercial vehicles and compliance with DOT regulations.

Procedure:

- Develop a maintenance schedule that adheres to DOT regulations, manufacturer recommendations, and the specific needs of your vehicles.

- Schedule routine vehicle inspections and maintenance checks, including pre-trip and post-trip inspections by drivers, and periodic thorough inspections by qualified mechanics.

- Conduct and document regular preventive maintenance tasks, such as oil changes, brake inspections, and tire rotations.

- Address and document any identified issues promptly and ensure repairs are made by qualified technicians.

Maintain maintenance records, including inspections, repairs, and servicing:

Importance: Proper record-keeping is essential for demonstrating compliance with DOT regulations and ensuring vehicle safety.

Procedure:

- Create a system for documenting all vehicle maintenance activities, including inspection reports, repairs, and servicing.

- Record details such as the date of maintenance, work performed, parts replaced, and the name of the technician or service provider.

- Keep records organized and easily accessible for inspection by authorities or auditors.

Ensure vehicles have the required safety equipment, such as reflective triangles, fire extinguishers, and first aid kits:

Importance: Equipping vehicles with necessary safety equipment is not only a regulatory requirement but also crucial for responding to emergencies and ensuring driver and public safety.

Procedure:

- Regularly inspect each vehicle to ensure it is equipped with mandatory safety items, including reflective triangles, fire extinguishers, and first aid kits.

- Check the condition and expiration dates of safety equipment to ensure they are current and functional.

- Replace or replenish safety equipment as needed, keeping extras on hand in case of emergencies.

General Tips:

- Conduct training sessions for drivers to ensure they understand the importance of pre-trip and post-trip inspections and can identify potential safety concerns.

- Establish a system for drivers to report any safety equipment issues or vehicle maintenance needs promptly.

- Consider implementing a computerized maintenance management system (CMMS) or fleet management software to help streamline maintenance and record-keeping processes.

- Regularly review and update your maintenance and inspection procedures to align with any changes in DOT regulations or industry best practices.

- Conduct surprise internal audits to ensure compliance with maintenance and safety equipment requirements.

By following these procedures and maintaining thorough records, your organization can ensure the safety of your fleet, demonstrate compliance with DOT regulations, and reduce the risk of accidents and violations during DOT audits and inspections.

4. Drug and Alcohol Testing

Confirm that your organization has a drug and alcohol testing program in place:

Importance: A drug and alcohol testing program is a crucial component of DOT compliance, helping to ensure that drivers and employees operate commercial vehicles safely and responsibly.

Procedure:

- Establish a written drug and alcohol testing policy that complies with DOT regulations and clearly communicates the program's expectations to employees.

- Appoint a designated employee (often a Substance Abuse Professional or SAP) responsible for overseeing the program's implementation and compliance.

- Ensure that all employees, including drivers and non-driving personnel, are aware of and understand the drug and alcohol testing program.

Keep records of pre-employment, random, and post-accident drug and alcohol test results:

Importance: Comprehensive record-keeping is essential for documenting compliance with DOT testing requirements and demonstrating that your organization takes drug and alcohol testing seriously.

Procedure:

- Maintain detailed records of all drug and alcohol tests, including pre-employment tests for new hires, random tests throughout the year, and post-accident tests conducted after certain types of accidents.

- Record test results, collection dates, locations, and the names of individuals tested.

- Keep records of any refusals to test and the reasons for these refusals.

- Store these records securely, ensuring they are easily accessible for DOT audits or inspections.

Ensure that all employees involved in drug and alcohol testing are trained and certified:

Importance: Properly trained and certified personnel are essential for conducting tests accurately, maintaining chain of custody, and ensuring the integrity of the testing process.

Procedure:

- Identify and designate qualified personnel to perform drug and alcohol testing, including collection site personnel, breath alcohol technicians (BATs), and urine specimen collectors.

- Ensure that these individuals receive proper training and certification through recognized organizations, such as the Substance Abuse Professional Administrators Association (SAPAA) or other relevant bodies.

- Maintain records of the certifications and training received by personnel involved in the testing process.

General Tips:

- Keep the drug and alcohol testing program consistent with DOT regulations, which specify testing percentages, testing types, and other requirements.

- Conduct annual supervisor training to educate those who oversee drivers about the signs and symptoms of substance abuse and how to handle reasonable suspicion testing.

- Implement a clear process for addressing positive test results, including rehabilitation and return-to-duty protocols.

- Review and update your drug and alcohol testing policy and procedures as needed to align with changes in regulations or industry best practices.

- Regularly audit your drug and alcohol testing program to identify areas for improvement and ensure ongoing compliance.

By following these procedures, your organization can maintain a robust drug and alcohol testing program, promote safety, and demonstrate compliance with DOT regulations during audits and inspections.

5. Safety Management and Policies

Develop and maintain a comprehensive safety policy that aligns with DOT regulations:

Importance: A well-defined safety policy sets the foundation for a safety-conscious organization and ensures alignment with DOT regulations, promoting the safety of both drivers and the public.

Procedure:

- Develop a written safety policy that covers all aspects of your operations, including driver behavior, vehicle maintenance, and compliance with DOT regulations.

- Ensure that the safety policy is easily accessible to all employees, and distribute copies to drivers and relevant personnel.

- Regularly review and update the policy to reflect changes in regulations, industry best practices, or incidents that highlight areas for improvement.

Conduct regular safety meetings and training sessions for drivers and staff:

Importance: Ongoing safety meetings and training sessions keep employees informed, engaged, and prepared to handle various safety-related situations.

Procedure:

- Schedule and conduct regular safety meetings with drivers and relevant staff members, focusing on topics such as HOS compliance, vehicle maintenance, defensive driving, and emergency response procedures.

- Use a variety of training methods, including classroom sessions, hands-on exercises, and online training, to engage employees and reinforce safety concepts.

- Encourage active participation and open discussions during safety meetings to address questions and concerns.

Keep records of safety meetings, training sessions, and safety-related communications:

Importance: Documenting safety-related activities and communications is crucial for demonstrating your organization's commitment to safety and compliance with DOT regulations.

Procedure:

- Maintain detailed records of all safety meetings, including dates, topics discussed, attendees, and any materials distributed.

- Record attendance and participation in training sessions and safety meetings to ensure that all employees receive the necessary training.

- Document any safety-related communications, such as safety bulletins, memos, or incident reports, and store them in an organized manner.

General Tips:

- Establish a safety committee or designate a safety manager responsible for overseeing safety-related activities and ensuring compliance with safety policies.

- Encourage a culture of safety by promoting reporting of safety concerns, near misses, and incidents, without fear of reprisal.

- Provide incentives or recognition for safe driving and adherence to safety policies to motivate employees to prioritize safety.

- Regularly evaluate the effectiveness of your safety program through safety audits, incident analysis, and feedback from employees.

- Use technology and training software to enhance safety training and record-keeping processes.

By implementing these procedures and maintaining comprehensive records of safety-related activities, your organization can demonstrate its commitment to safety, ensure compliance with DOT regulations, and promote a safer work environment for drivers and staff.

6. Vehicle Records and Documentation

Maintain vehicle registration and insurance documents, and ensure they are up to date:

Importance: Proper vehicle registration and insurance documentation are essential to demonstrate compliance with legal requirements and ensure that your vehicles are legally allowed on the road.

Procedure:

Vehicle Registration:

- Keep copies of the vehicle registration for each vehicle in your fleet. Ensure that the registrations are up to date and renewed before expiration.

- Regularly check registration expiration dates and establish a renewal process to prevent lapses in registration.

Vehicle Insurance:

- Maintain copies of the insurance policies for all vehicles. Ensure that the coverage meets the minimum requirements set by DOT regulations.

- Keep insurance policies up to date and renew them promptly. Verify that your organization is listed as the insured party.

Keep copies of vehicle titles, lease agreements, and any other relevant vehicle ownership records:

Importance: Vehicle ownership records are essential for proving ownership and legal authority over the vehicles in your fleet. Lease agreements are important for leased vehicles.

Procedure:

Vehicle Titles:

- Maintain copies of vehicle titles for all owned vehicles. These documents prove legal ownership and may be required during DOT audits or inspections.

- Keep titles in a secure and easily accessible location, and update them if there are any changes in ownership.

Lease Agreements:

- If your organization leases vehicles, keep copies of lease agreements for each leased vehicle. These agreements should outline responsibilities and compliance requirements.

- Ensure that lease agreements are up to date and align with DOT regulations and insurance requirements.

General Tips:

- Establish a systematic approach to document management, organizing records by vehicle identification number (VIN) or license plate for easy retrieval.

- Regularly review all vehicle documentation to verify that it is current and compliant with DOT regulations.

- Implement a process for updating documentation promptly when there are changes in vehicle ownership or insurance coverage.

- Provide access to these documents for relevant personnel, such as those responsible for fleet management, compliance, and auditing.

- Consider digitizing your vehicle records and storing them securely in a cloud-based system to enhance accessibility and backup capabilities.

By following these procedures, your organization can maintain accurate and up-to-date vehicle records and documentation, which is crucial for ensuring compliance with DOT regulations and providing the necessary documentation during audits or inspections.

7. Incident and Accident Reports

Maintain records of all accidents, incidents, and near misses.

Importance: Keeping detailed records of accidents, incidents, and near misses is crucial for safety improvement, liability protection, and compliance with DOT regulations.

Procedure:

Accident Reports:

- Whenever an accident occurs involving one of your commercial vehicles, create an accident report. Include information such as the date, time, location, weather conditions, vehicle involved, drivers' details, and a description of the accident.

- Document any injuries, fatalities, or property damage resulting from the accident.

- File a report with the appropriate authorities as required by local, state, and federal regulations.

- **Incident Reports:**

- Record all incidents that don't result in accidents but still involve safety concerns or potential violations. This could include equipment malfunctions, unsafe driving behavior, or non-compliance with safety protocols.

- Include similar details as accident reports, such as date, time, location, involved parties, and descriptions of the incident.

Near Miss Reports:

- Encourage drivers and staff to report near misses, which are situations where an accident or incident almost occurred but was narrowly avoided.

- Document these reports in the same manner as incidents and accidents to identify patterns or potential risks.

Investigate accidents and incidents to identify causes and preventive measures:

- Importance: Investigating accidents and incidents helps uncover root causes, allowing for corrective actions to prevent similar occurrences in the future and enhance safety.

Procedure:

Prompt Investigation:

- After an accident or incident occurs, initiate a prompt and thorough investigation. Interview involved parties, gather evidence, and assess the scene.

Root Cause Analysis:

- Determine the underlying causes of the accident or incident. It may involve factors such as driver behavior, equipment failure, external conditions, or procedural shortcomings.

- Analyze data from telematics, driver logs, and other sources to identify contributing factors.

Corrective Actions:

- Develop and implement corrective actions and preventive measures based on the investigation findings. These actions may include changes to policies and procedures, additional training, equipment maintenance, or disciplinary measures.

Documentation:

- Maintain detailed records of the investigation process, findings, and actions taken to prevent recurrence.

General Tips:

- Create a culture that encourages open reporting of accidents, incidents, and near misses without fear of reprisal, as this promotes safety improvement.

- Use incident and accident reports as learning opportunities to enhance safety training and risk mitigation.

- Regularly review accident and incident data to identify trends and areas for improvement.

- Train staff and drivers on the importance of accurate and timely reporting and the role it plays in overall safety.

By following these procedures, your organization can effectively manage and learn from accidents, incidents, and near misses, helping to improve safety and reduce the likelihood of future incidents. Additionally, it demonstrates a commitment to safety, which is essential for compliance with DOT regulations.

8. Emergency Response Plan

Develop and maintain an emergency response plan for accidents or hazardous situations:

Importance: An emergency response plan is essential for ensuring that your organization can effectively and safely manage accidents, incidents, or hazardous situations, thereby minimizing harm and damage.

Procedure:

Risk Assessment:

- Conduct a thorough risk assessment to identify potential emergencies or hazardous situations specific to your operations. Consider factors such as geographic location, cargo type, and common challenges.

Plan Development:

- Develop a comprehensive emergency response plan that outlines specific procedures and protocols for responding to various scenarios. The plan should cover accidents, spills, fires, medical emergencies, and more.

- Specify roles and responsibilities for employees during an emergency. Assign tasks such as calling emergency services, providing first aid, and managing evacuations.

- Ensure the plan is in compliance with DOT regulations and any other relevant local, state, or federal requirements.

Communication:

- Establish communication protocols, including how to notify authorities, emergency services, and affected parties.

- Include contact information for key personnel, emergency services, and regulatory agencies in the plan.

Resources:

- Identify and list the resources required to manage emergencies, including first aid kits, fire extinguishers, personal protective equipment (PPE), spill containment materials, and more.

- Ensure these resources are readily available and properly maintained.

Training and Drills:

- Develop a training program that covers the emergency response plan. Train employees, including drivers, on their roles and responsibilities during emergencies.

- Conduct regular drills and exercises to test the effectiveness of the plan and ensure that employees are well-prepared for real-life emergencies.

Train drivers and employees on the emergency response plan:

Importance: Proper training ensures that all employees, including drivers, know how to respond effectively to emergencies, reducing the potential for injuries, environmental damage, and regulatory violations.

Procedure:

Initial Training:

- Provide comprehensive training to all employees, including new hires, on the emergency response plan during onboarding.

- Cover key aspects of the plan, including reporting procedures, evacuation routes, first aid, and use of emergency equipment.

Regular Refresher Training:

- Conduct periodic refresher training sessions to keep employees updated on the plan and any changes or updates.

- Include scenario-based training to simulate emergency situations and test employees' responses.

Driver-Specific Training:

- For drivers, emphasize their roles in emergencies, such as securing the vehicle, assessing the safety of the scene, and providing assistance to injured parties if safe to do so.

- Train drivers on how to safely transport hazardous materials in the event of a spill or accident.

General Tips:

- Ensure that the emergency response plan is accessible to all employees, both digitally and in print form.

- Establish a chain of command for emergencies, designating a primary and secondary point of contact for each role or responsibility.

- Periodically review and update the emergency response plan based on lessons learned from drills, exercises, and real-life incidents.

- Collaborate with local emergency services and regulatory agencies to ensure alignment with their response protocols and requirements.

- Encourage employees to report any safety concerns or potential hazards that could lead to emergencies.

By following these procedures, your organization can be well-prepared to respond effectively to emergencies, protect the safety of employees and the public, and demonstrate compliance with DOT regulations related to emergency response planning and training.

9. Compliance with Hazmat Regulations (if applicable)

Ensure compliance with Hazardous Materials (Hazmat) regulations, if your organization transports hazardous materials:

Importance: Transporting hazardous materials poses unique risks and legal obligations, making it essential to comply with Hazmat regulations to protect the safety of individuals, property, and the environment.

Procedure:

Determine Applicability:

- Identify whether your organization transports hazardous materials under DOT regulations. Hazmat materials are classified based on their potential hazards, such as flammability, toxicity, corrosiveness, or radioactivity.

- Determine the specific regulations that apply to the type and quantity of hazardous materials you transport.

Hazmat Transportation Plan:

- Develop a Hazmat transportation plan that includes detailed procedures for the safe handling, packaging, labeling, placarding, and emergency response for hazardous materials.

- Ensure that all employees, especially drivers, are aware of and trained in the specific requirements for the Hazmat materials they handle.

- **Proper Documentation:**

- Complete and maintain all required documentation, such as shipping papers, manifests, placards, and labels, in accordance with Hazmat regulations.

- Verify that hazardous materials are properly packaged and labeled before transport.

Security Measures:

- Implement security measures to prevent unauthorized access to Hazmat materials during transport. Hazmat security plans may be required for certain materials.

Emergency Response:

- Include procedures for responding to Hazmat incidents in your emergency response plan, including actions to protect employees, the public, and the environment in the event of a spill, leak, or other Hazmat emergency.

Maintain Hazmat training records for drivers and employees:

Importance: Hazmat training is crucial for ensuring that employees, especially drivers, are aware of the risks associated with hazardous materials and can handle them safely and in compliance with regulations.

Procedure:

Identify Training Needs:

- Determine which employees require Hazmat training based on their roles and responsibilities. This typically includes drivers, loaders, and anyone involved in the transportation or handling of hazardous materials.

Training Programs:

- Enroll employees in Hazmat training programs that meet the requirements outlined in 49 CFR Part 172, Subpart H. Training should cover topics such as Hazmat classification, labeling, placarding, packaging, and emergency response.

Record Keeping:

- Maintain detailed training records for each employee, including documentation of training completion, dates, topics covered, and the name of the trainer.

- Ensure that training records are readily accessible and kept for the required retention period.

Refresher Training:

- Conduct periodic Hazmat refresher training to ensure that employees stay up to date with the latest regulations and best practices.

- Provide additional training if there are changes in job responsibilities or regulations.

General Tips:

- Use DOT Hazmat regulations (49 CFR Parts 171-180) as a primary reference for compliance requirements.

- Regularly review and update your Hazmat transportation plan and training materials to align with regulatory changes and industry best practices.

- Collaborate with Hazmat authorities and industry organizations to stay informed about updates and changes to Hazmat regulations.

- Ensure that your Hazmat emergency response plan aligns with other emergency response plans in your organization, promoting coordination during Hazmat incidents.

By following these procedures, your organization can maintain compliance with Hazmat regulations, enhance the safety of Hazmat transportation, and reduce the risk of incidents, accidents, and violations during DOT audits and inspections related to Hazmat materials.

10. Record Retention

Establish a record retention policy to retain all relevant documents for the required time periods:

Importance: Proper record retention is vital for ensuring compliance with DOT regulations, responding to audits, and maintaining organized documentation of your operations.

Procedure:

Identify Applicable Regulations:

- Review DOT regulations, industry standards, and legal requirements to determine the specific record retention periods applicable to your organization. These periods can vary based on the type of document and its purpose.

Create a Record Retention Policy:

- Develop a comprehensive record retention policy that outlines which documents must be retained, how long they should be kept, and how they should be stored.

- Ensure that the policy aligns with all relevant regulations, covering areas such as driver qualification files, maintenance records, accident reports, and more.

Retention Periods:

- Establish clear guidelines for document retention periods. Some examples include retaining driver qualification files for three years, vehicle maintenance records for one year, and accident reports for five years.

- Differentiate between electronic and physical records, as some regulations specify different retention periods for each.

Secure Storage:

- Determine the appropriate storage method for your records, taking into consideration factors such as security, accessibility, and preservation.

- Ensure that electronic records are backed up and protected against data loss or corruption.

Ensure easy and organized access to records for auditors:

Importance: During DOT audits and inspections, having organized and easily accessible records can facilitate the process, demonstrate compliance, and help avoid potential penalties.

Procedure:

Organized Recordkeeping:

- Establish a system for organizing and categorizing records based on their type and retention period. Create separate folders or digital storage locations for different types of documents.

- Use clear and standardized naming conventions for electronic files to make searching and retrieval easier.

Documentation Index:

- Develop an index or catalog of all retained records, including details such as the document type, date range, location, and responsible personnel.

- Ensure that this index is regularly updated as new records are added and old records reach their expiration dates.

Auditor Accessibility:

- Designate a specific location or a responsible individual who can provide auditors with access to the requested records promptly.

- Ensure that auditors have access to both physical and electronic records as needed, along with any necessary tools or software to view electronic records.

General Tips:

- Periodically review and update your record retention policy to ensure that it remains in compliance with changing regulations and industry standards.

- Train relevant personnel on the importance of proper record retention, document organization, and their roles in facilitating audits or inspections.

- Consider using document management software or electronic record-keeping systems to streamline organization and accessibility.

- Conduct regular internal audits or self-assessments of your record-keeping practices to identify and address any deficiencies or non-compliance issues.

- Retain records beyond the minimum required period if there is a potential for future litigation or if it aligns with your organization's risk management strategy.

By following these procedures, your organization can effectively manage record retention, ensuring compliance with DOT regulations, facilitating audits and inspections, and promoting an organized and efficient record-keeping system.

11. Mock Audit and Training

Conduct regular mock DOT audits to identify and rectify compliance issues:

Importance: Conducting mock DOT audits helps your organization proactively identify and address compliance issues, reducing the risk of violations during actual DOT audits and inspections.

Procedure:

Audit Preparation:

- Simulate a DOT audit by selecting a team or auditor to review your organization's records, policies, and procedures.

- Use a comprehensive DOT audit checklist that covers all relevant areas, including driver qualification files, vehicle maintenance, hours of service, and more.

Audit Process:

- Conduct the mock audit as realistically as possible, including reviewing records, interviewing personnel, and assessing compliance with DOT regulations.

- Identify any deficiencies, errors, or gaps in compliance during the mock audit.

Issue Resolution:

- After the mock audit, compile a list of findings and deficiencies. Prioritize these issues based on their severity and potential impact on compliance.

- Develop corrective action plans for each issue, assigning responsibilities and deadlines for resolution.

Re-Audit:

- Conduct a follow-up mock audit to assess whether the identified issues have been effectively addressed and corrected.

- Use the results of the re-audit to confirm that the corrective actions have been successful.

Provide ongoing training and education to staff and drivers to stay updated on DOT regulations:

Importance: Regular training and education are essential to ensure that staff and drivers are aware of and compliant with the latest DOT regulations and industry best practices.

Procedure:

Training Needs Assessment:

- Identify the training needs of your organization by considering factors such as changes in regulations, employee turnover, and evolving industry standards.

Training Programs:

- Develop and deliver training programs that address the identified needs. Training topics may include HOS compliance, Hazmat handling, safety procedures, and more.

- Offer both initial training for new employees and ongoing refresher training for existing staff and drivers.

- **Regulatory Updates:**

- Stay informed about updates to DOT regulations, guidance documents, and enforcement priorities. Use official DOT resources, industry publications, and training materials.

Driver Communication:

- Regularly communicate with drivers about regulatory changes, safety reminders, and any new training requirements.

- Encourage drivers to ask questions and report concerns related to compliance or safety.

General Tips:

- Consider using technology, such as e-learning platforms or webinars, to facilitate training and education for geographically dispersed staff and drivers.

- Encourage a culture of continuous learning and improvement, where employees are engaged in ongoing education and contribute to compliance efforts.

- Establish a feedback mechanism for employees to provide input on training programs and suggest areas for improvement.

- Document all training activities, including attendance records, training materials, and assessments, to demonstrate compliance with DOT training requirements.

- Collaborate with industry organizations and associations to access training resources, share best practices, and stay informed about regulatory developments.

By following these procedures, your organization can proactively address compliance issues, enhance staff and driver knowledge, and reduce the risk of violations during actual DOT audits and inspections. Additionally, it helps promote a culture of safety and regulatory compliance within your organization.

12. Compliance Review by Legal Counsel

Engage legal counsel or compliance experts to periodically review your operations for DOT compliance:

Importance: Seeking legal counsel or compliance experts to review your operations for DOT compliance is a proactive approach to ensure that your organization remains in adherence to all applicable regulations. Legal professionals and compliance experts possess the expertise needed to identify potential issues and provide guidance on corrective actions.

Procedure:

Legal Counsel Selection:

- Identify legal counsel or compliance experts with expertise in DOT regulations and transportation law. Look for professionals or firms experienced in representing transportation companies or providing compliance consulting services.

- Consider referrals, industry associations, and reviews when choosing legal counsel or experts.

Scope of Review:

- Define the scope of the compliance review, specifying which areas of DOT regulations and operations will be examined. This may include driver qualifications, hours of service, vehicle maintenance, Hazmat compliance, record-keeping, and more.

- Discuss your organization's specific concerns or areas where you suspect potential compliance issues.

Review Process:

- Collaborate closely with legal counsel or compliance experts during the review process. Provide access to records, policies, and personnel as needed.

- Allow experts to conduct a comprehensive assessment of your operations, records, and procedures related to DOT compliance.

- Encourage open communication and questions during the review process.

Findings and Recommendations:

- After the review, legal counsel or compliance experts will provide a report detailing their findings. This report may include identified compliance issues, potential liabilities, and areas for improvement.

- Request specific recommendations for addressing any compliance deficiencies or issues uncovered during the review.

Corrective Actions:

- Implement corrective actions based on the recommendations provided by legal counsel or compliance experts. Assign responsibilities, establish timelines, and monitor progress.

- Seek guidance from legal counsel on addressing any legal issues or liabilities identified during the review.

Ongoing Collaboration:

- Establish an ongoing relationship with legal counsel or compliance experts to ensure continued support and guidance as regulations evolve or your operations change.

- Schedule periodic follow-up reviews to assess the effectiveness of corrective actions and to ensure ongoing compliance.

General Tips:

- Prioritize transparency and cooperation with legal counsel or compliance experts. Share all relevant information, even if it may reveal areas of non-compliance.

- Maintain attorney-client privilege when discussing legal matters with counsel to protect sensitive information.

- Keep abreast of regulatory changes and updates in the transportation industry to ensure that your compliance efforts remain current.

- Communicate with your legal counsel regarding any legal challenges or regulatory inquiries your organization may face, and seek their guidance on the best course of action.

By engaging legal counsel or compliance experts to periodically review your operations for DOT compliance, you can gain valuable insights, proactively address compliance issues, and minimize legal and regulatory risks, ultimately promoting a culture of compliance within your organization.

13. Corrective Action Plan

Develop a corrective action plan to address any deficiencies or violations discovered during self-audits or mock audits:

Importance: A corrective action plan is essential for addressing and rectifying deficiencies or violations identified during self-audits or mock DOT audits. It outlines the steps your organization will take to bring operations back into compliance with DOT regulations.

Procedure:

Deficiency Identification:

- Begin by reviewing the findings of your self-audit or mock DOT audit to identify specific deficiencies, violations, or areas of non-compliance with DOT regulations.

Prioritization:

- Prioritize the identified deficiencies based on their severity, potential impact on safety, and regulatory importance. Focus on addressing the most critical issues first.

Root Cause Analysis:

- For each deficiency, conduct a root cause analysis to determine why the issue occurred. Understand the underlying factors contributing to the non-compliance.

Corrective Actions:

- Develop a set of specific corrective actions for each identified deficiency. These actions should be detailed, actionable, and designed to address the root causes.

- Assign responsibilities for each corrective action, specifying who will be responsible for implementing and overseeing the action.

Timelines and Milestones:

- Establish clear timelines and milestones for completing each corrective action. Ensure that the timelines are realistic and achievable.

Resources:

Identify the resources, including personnel, training, equipment, or technology, needed to implement the corrective actions successfully.

Monitoring and Validation:

- Implement a monitoring and validation process to track the progress of each corrective action. Verify that the actions are completed as planned and are effective in addressing the deficiencies.

Documentation:

- Maintain thorough documentation of the entire corrective action process, including the identified deficiencies, root cause analyses, corrective actions, progress updates, and final outcomes.

Communication:

- Communicate the corrective action plan to all relevant stakeholders within your organization. Ensure that employees are aware of their roles and responsibilities in the plan's execution.

General Tips:

- Foster a culture of accountability and responsibility within your organization to ensure that corrective actions are implemented effectively.

- Regularly update and review the status of the corrective action plan to ensure that all deficiencies are addressed in a timely manner.

- Consider involving cross-functional teams or subject matter experts in the development and execution of corrective actions to bring a diverse perspective to problem-solving.

- Engage with legal counsel or compliance experts if necessary to ensure that corrective actions align with legal requirements and regulatory expectations.

- Use lessons learned from the corrective action process to improve policies, procedures, and training to prevent similar issues from arising in the future.

By following these procedures, your organization can develop and implement an effective corrective action plan to address deficiencies or violations discovered during self-audits or mock DOT audits. This helps ensure compliance with DOT regulations, promotes safety, and minimizes the risk of regulatory penalties or enforcement actions.

14. Document Management

Implement a robust document management system to store and organize all DOT-related records:

Importance: Effective document management is essential for maintaining compliance with DOT regulations, facilitating audits and inspections, and ensuring that records are organized, accessible, and secure.

Procedure:

Assessment:

- Begin by assessing your organization's current document management practices, including how records are stored, organized, and accessed. Identify any deficiencies or areas for improvement.

Select a Document Management System:

- Choose a suitable document management system (DMS) or software that meets your organization's needs. The DMS should be capable of handling electronic and physical records, offer robust search and retrieval features, and provide security controls.

Document Categorization:

- Establish a systematic method for categorizing and organizing documents. Create standardized folders, tags, or metadata that align with DOT-related categories such as driver qualification files, vehicle maintenance records, and incident reports.

Document Digitization:

- Digitize paper records and documents as much as possible. Use scanning technology to convert physical records into electronic formats. Ensure that scanned documents are of high quality and clarity.

Access Control:

- Implement access controls and permissions within the DMS to restrict access to sensitive or confidential documents. Assign access rights based on job roles and responsibilities.

Data Retention:

- Configure the DMS to enforce document retention periods based on DOT regulations and organizational policies. Ensure that documents are automatically archived or deleted when their retention periods expire.

Version Control:

- Maintain version control for documents that may undergo revisions or updates. Track changes and ensure that the latest versions are readily accessible to authorized personnel.

Backup and Disaster Recovery:

- Implement regular backups of electronic documents to prevent data loss in case of technical failures or disasters. Establish a disaster recovery plan for document recovery in emergencies.

Training and User Adoption:

- Provide training to employees on how to use the DMS effectively. Ensure that staff understand how to upload, retrieve, and manage documents within the system.

General Tips:

- Regularly review and update your document management policies and procedures to keep them aligned with regulatory changes and evolving best practices.

- Conduct periodic audits or checks of the DMS to ensure that documents are accurately categorized, properly retained, and easily retrievable.

- Encourage employees to report any issues or challenges they encounter with the DMS, and consider their feedback for system improvements.

- Maintain a backup system or secure off-site storage for physical records to prevent loss in the event of physical damage or disasters.

- Ensure that the DMS complies with data protection and privacy regulations, especially when handling sensitive employee information.

By following these procedures, your organization can implement an effective document management system that simplifies compliance with DOT regulations, improves operational efficiency, and ensures that all DOT-related records are organized, secure, and readily accessible when needed.

15. Communication Protocol

Establish a communication protocol for interacting with DOT auditors during an actual audit:

Importance: Having a well-defined communication protocol in place is crucial when facing an actual DOT audit. It helps ensure a smooth and organized audit process, enhances transparency, and promotes compliance with regulatory requirements.

Procedure:

Pre-Audit Preparation:

- Designate a point person or team responsible for coordinating communication with DOT auditors. This individual or team should be knowledgeable about the organization's operations and DOT compliance requirements.

Contact Information:

- Ensure that you have up-to-date contact information for the DOT auditors who will be conducting the audit. This information typically includes their names, phone numbers, email addresses, and any additional contact details provided by the auditors or their agency.

Primary Contact:

- Designate a primary contact person within your organization who will serve as the main point of communication with the auditors. This individual should be available throughout the audit process.

Document Sharing:

- Establish a secure method for sharing requested documents with auditors. This may involve providing physical copies of records or granting access to electronic records through a secure portal.

Opening Meeting:

- Schedule an opening meeting with the auditors at the beginning of the audit. During this meeting, introduce key personnel, review the audit scope and objectives, and establish expectations for communication throughout the audit.

Document Requests:

- Designate a responsible individual or team within your organization for promptly gathering and providing requested documents to the auditors. Maintain a record of all documents provided, including dates and copies of submitted materials.

Question and Clarification Process:

- Establish a process for addressing any questions or requests for clarification from the auditors. Responses should be accurate and provided in a timely manner.

Audit Progress Updates:

- Maintain regular communication with the auditors to provide updates on the progress of the audit, including any challenges or delays that may arise.

Closing Meeting:

- Schedule a closing meeting with the auditors at the conclusion of the audit. Review findings, discuss any identified deficiencies or violations, and confirm next steps and timelines for corrective actions.

Follow-Up Communication:

- Determine how follow-up communication will be handled after the audit. This may involve additional document requests, clarifications, or updates on corrective actions.

General Tips:

- Familiarize yourself with the specific audit process and requirements of the DOT agency conducting the audit, as procedures may vary among different agencies.

- Maintain a professional and cooperative demeanor when communicating with auditors, as this can positively influence the audit experience.

- Train relevant staff on their roles and responsibilities in supporting the communication protocol during the audit.

- Retain records of all communications with auditors, including meeting notes, email correspondence, and any additional documentation related to the audit.

- Seek legal counsel or compliance experts' guidance in case of complex or legally sensitive audit matters.

By following these procedures, your organization can establish an effective communication protocol for interacting with DOT auditors during an actual audit, ensuring a well-organized, transparent, and compliant audit process.

Resources and Useful Links

In the realm of fleet compliance, having the right resources and information at your fingertips can make all the difference. This chapter serves as an invaluable appendix, providing a curated collection of web links to relevant regulatory agencies, industry associations, and online tools that can aid fleet managers and professionals in their ongoing journey towards compliance excellence.

Regulatory Agencies

These links connect you to federal and state regulatory agencies responsible for overseeing and enforcing compliance regulations:

- **Federal Motor Carrier Safety Administration (FMCSA):** https://www.fmcsa.dot.gov/

- **U.S. Department of Transportation (DOT):** https://www.transportation.gov/

- **Environmental Protection Agency (EPA):** https://www.epa.gov/

- **Occupational Safety and Health Administration (OSHA):** https://www.osha.gov/

Industry Associations

These associations provide valuable resources, updates, and networking opportunities within the commercial motor carrier industry:

- **American Trucking Associations (ATA):** https://www.trucking.org/

- **National Private Truck Council (NPTC):** https://www.nptc.org/

- **Transportation Intermediaries Association (TIA):** https://www.tianet.org/

- **National Association of Small Trucking Companies (NASTC):** https://nastc.com/

Online Compliance Tools

These online tools can aid in various aspects of fleet compliance management:

- **KeepTruckin (ELD and Fleet Management):** https://keeptruckin.com/

- **Geotab (Telematics and Fleet Management):** https://www.geotab.com/

- **Samsara (IoT Solutions for Fleet Management):** https://www.samsara.com/

- **JJ Keller DataSense (Driver Qualification Management):** https://www.jjkellers.com/datasense

Compliance Resources and Training

These resources offer compliance training, guides, and valuable insights:

- **FMCSA Online Learning Center:** https://www.fmcsa.dot.gov/learning-center

- **Safety & Compliance Training by J. J. Keller:** https://www.jjkellers.com/learn

- **National Safety Council (NSC) Fleet Driver Training:** https://www.nsc.org/road-safety/safety-topics/fleet-driver-safety

- **FMCSA Regulatory Guidance:** https://www.fmcsa.dot.gov/regulations/guidance

Compliance Software and Solutions

These software solutions cater to various aspects of fleet compliance:

- **Verizon Connect (Telematics and Fleet Management):** https://www.verizonconnect.com/

- **Samsara (IoT Solutions for Fleet Management):** https://www.samsara.com/

- **Omnitracs (Fleet Management and Telematics):** https://www.omnitracs.com/

- **Transporeon (Logistics and Transportation Management):** https://www.transporeon.com/

Regulatory Updates and News

Stay informed about the latest regulatory changes and industry news:

- **Transport Topics (Transportation News):** https://www.ttnews.com/

- **Overdrive (Trucking News):**
  https://www.overdriveonline.com/

- **Fleet Owner (Fleet Management News):**
  https://www.fleetowner.com/

Forums and Community Platforms

Engage with industry peers and experts, share experiences, and seek advice:

- **The Truckers Report Forum:**
  https://www.thetruckersreport.com/truckingindustryforum/

- **TruckersMP (Trucking Multiplayer Community):**
  https://truckersmp.com/